Machines at work

Harvesters

AXIS education

Acknowledgements

Photographs: pages 3 and 7 © Case; page 4 © PMC; pages 5, 6, 10 and 37 © John Deere; pages 7, 15 and 17 © David Wright; page 7 © AGCO; page 8 © Valtra; page 9 © Claas; page 11 © Bruce Guenter; page 12 © Robert Scarth; page 13 © Massey Ferguson; page 18 © Tonny Hoste; page 19 © Werktuigdagen; page 21 © Ingo Bernhardt and © Kim Haws; page 23 © Ellen Meiselman www.thedesignspace.net; page 25 © T P Martins; page 26 © Meghan Rutherford; page 27 © Washington State University/Carol Ann Mills; pages 28, 29 and 33 © Keith Weller and the US Agricultural Research Service; page 31 © Robert Pitkin; page 35 © Natalie Maynor.

Every effort has been made to contact copyright holders of material reproduced in this book. Any omissions will be rectified in subsequent printings if notice is given to the publishers.

Copyright © Axis Education 2012

All rights reserved; no part of this publication may be reproduced, stored in a retrieval system, transmitted in any form, or by any means, electronic, mechanical, photocopying, recording or otherwise, without the prior permission of the publisher.

First published in Great Britain by Axis Education Ltd.

ISBN 978-1-84618-300-3

Axis Education
PO Box 459
Shrewsbury
SY4 4WZ

Email: enquiries@axiseducation.co.uk

www.axiseducation.co.uk

A harvester is a farm machine to harvest crops. The most popular harvester is a combine harvester. You'll see these very busy in the fields at the end of the summer.

A Case machine hard at work.

Machines at work

The most common harvesting machines are combine harvesters for grain crops and forage harvesters for hay and straw. There are all sorts of other harvesters too. They tend to be used in large-scale operations. Wine growing countries often use grape harvesters to pick grapes. In East Anglia in the UK very large fields grow peas for the frozen pea industry. These fields are often picked with a special pea harvester.

A pea harvester ready for action.

Before farms had machines lots of workers were needed to gather the crops at harvest time. For cereal crops, the workers had to do a series of jobs to get the crops ready. They had to cut the plants, usually with a knife called a scythe. Then they separated the grain by threshing the cut stalks. Finally they cleaned away any debris around the seeds before the grain went to the mill for grinding. The whole process was very time consuming.

These days combine harvesters do all of these jobs with just one machine. They are called combine harvesters because they combine all of the jobs – harvesting, threshing and grain cleaning. All the combine driver has to do is drive the machine across the field and the machine will cut, thresh and clean the grain as it goes.

The combine harvester – harvests, threshes and cleans the grain.

Machines at work

As the harvester travels over the crop it is gathered in by the header. A reel pushes the crop down to the cutter bar which chops off the plants quite close to the ground.

Gathering the crop in the header.

The view from the combine cab.

The cut cereal moves up a conveyor belt to the threshing drum where the grain is shaken off the stalks. The grain drops through a sieve to a tank called a hopper. The waste material, known as chaff and straw, is pushed out of the back of the harvester.

The chaff and straw come out of the back of the combine.

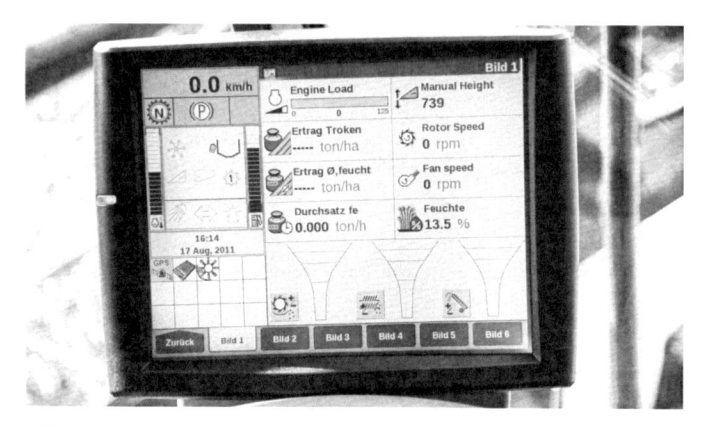

Clever computers help the combine driver.

Machines at work

When the hopper is full, the driver empties it into a waiting trailer. The grain is carried up from the tank and is shot out into the trailer from a side pipe.

Trailers work alongside the combine ready for the grain.

There are several contenders for most powerful combine harvester. Until recently the Claas Lexion 770 was probably the biggest machine in the world. Now John Deere, the world's biggest manufacturer of combines, has created the S690. This machine has the most powerful engine in a combine today. Its twin turbo-charged S series PowerTech PSX 13.5 litre engine has a massive 625 horsepower.

No longer the world's biggest combine, the Claas Lexion 770 is still a beast of a machine.

Machines at work

The S690 also has a 10 tonne capacity, making this the largest grain tank too. So the driver can work longer before stopping to empty the load. What's more, when the tank is full the grain can be emptied in just 105 seconds. The S-Series can travel on the road at a top speed of 18mph. Those who have driven it say that the machine is bigger, faster and better at its job than other machines. It's also easy to use and is very comfortable – it even has a fridge to keep the driver's lunch cool.

The world's biggest combine harvester – John Deere S690.

Forage harvesters are machines for making hay and straw for animal feed. Before the forage harvester can get to work a tractor mows the crop. It is left to dry lying in swaths, or rows.

Swaths of grass drying before being harvested.

Machines at work

Once the grass has dried, the forage harvester gathers it, chops it up and drops the cut grass or straw into a waiting trailer.

A Claas forage harvester gathering hay.

Harvesters

If the crop that's been harvested is grass, it will be taken away to be made into silage. Otherwise it will be collected up and baled with a baling machine.

This machine makes square bales.

Machines at work

Potatoes are harvested with a special machine. The whole plant is lifted out of the ground. Then a series of chains shake any soil from the potatoes and separate the stalks and leaves of the plant. The soil and leaves drop back onto the field. The clean potatoes travel up a conveyor belt and drop into a waiting trailer.

Depending on how many potatoes need to be harvested, a farmer might use a tractor-pulled machine that will work on a single row of potatoes at a time, or a dedicated machine that can lift up to six rows at once.

Timing the harvest depends on the weather. Potatoes need to be harvested at certain temperatures to make sure they can be stored for a long time. If the temperature is too warm, the potatoes may go bad. If the temperature is too cool, the potatoes will be bruised during the harvest.

Harvesters

Work on this potato field is nearly done.

Machines at work

A British company, PNC, make a world-class machine for harvesting peas. The 979CT can also be adapted to harvest other vegetables that grow in pods, such as beans. PNC sell this monster machine worldwide because it is so good at its job.

At the front of the 979CT is a roller with prongs that rotate. These prongs strip off the pod and part of the vine. The pods move on belts inside the machine to a threshing drum. This drum has five beaters that thresh the pods at just the right pressure to remove the peas from the pods without damaging them.

The peas are sieved and pass through a cleaning fan on their way to the top of the machine. Any unthreshed peas are taken out before the peas drop into the 3.1m^3 hopper. The six-wheel drive machine can also be tracked if it needs to work in very wet conditions. At 4 metres tall, over 11 metres long and 4 metres wide, this is a monster of a machine.

Harvesters

Pea harvesters on their way home after a long day in the field.

Machines at work

There are specialist harvesters for many vegetables. Leek harvesters work with long lifting arms that lift up the leeks between two belts. Soil is cleaned away with two shakers without damaging the leeks. They are strong machines capable of working in harsh, cold and muddy conditions.

Harvesting leeks.

Harvesters

Cabbage harvesters work by lifting the cabbage out of the ground with two torpedoes, folding the outer leaves over the cabbage to protect it. The cabbages are held by a clip that moves up a conveyor belt. The sides of the clip are made of rubber so the cabbage doesn't bruise. Underneath the belt a knife cuts off the roots and excess leaves. At the end of the belt, workers collect the cabbages and place them into containers or crates.

Cabbage harvesters taking a break.

Machines at work

You really need to know that asparagus is ripe before you pick it, so it is one crop that has always been hard to harvest with a machine. Experts have been trying to invent an asparagus harvester that works since 1908. A company in America called Haws may be nearly there.

The problem has been that while hand pickers can tell whether or not the vegetable is ripe a machine can't. Each spear of an asparagus plant matures at a different speed, so it is difficult to get an even harvest. The new Haws Harvester can go through a field at 4 miles per hour and pick all the spears that are tall enough, but it leaves unripe spears to be picked when they're ready.

The harvester works with a light-beam sensor. When the machine goes over a row of plants, the taller spears trip the sensor. Those spears are cut and put onto a conveyor belt. They go up the belt to a sorting table on top of the machine. Human workers then sort the harvest.

Harvesters

The machine costs £200,000 but large asparagus farms are keen to get their hands on it because it will save them time and money.

Asparagus grows at different rates.

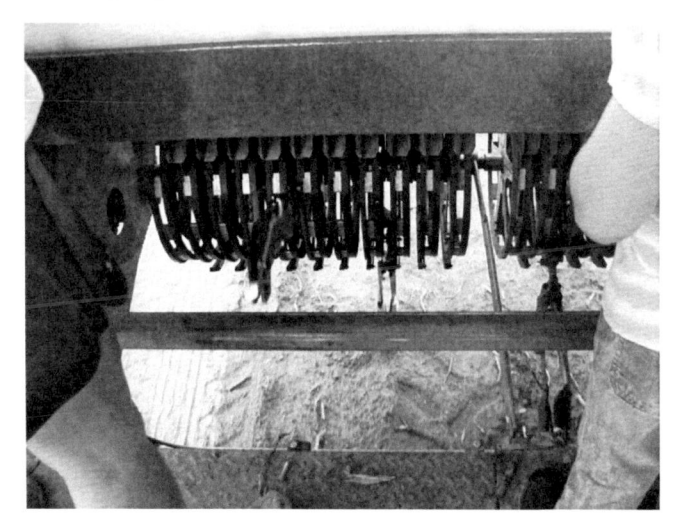

With this new machine hand-harvesting could be a thing of the past.

Machines at work

In countries where tomatoes are grown for canning or ketchup, farmers grow the crop in enormous fields and use special machines to harvest the fruit.

Earlier tomato harvesters were towed by a tractor. Newer harvesters are a complete machine that works by driving over each row of tomatoes. It uses a cutting bar to remove the main plant from the roots. A conveyor belt brings the tomatoes inside the machine where they are shaken off the vines. Then the fruit is sorted electronically. Clods of earth and unripe tomatoes are pushed back onto the ground and will be used to make fertiliser for future tomato crops.

Human labour is still used to pick out anything that may have been missed by the scanners, but fewer workers are needed than with the older, towed harvesting machines. A new tomato harvester with electronic sorters costs over £240,000.

Harvesters

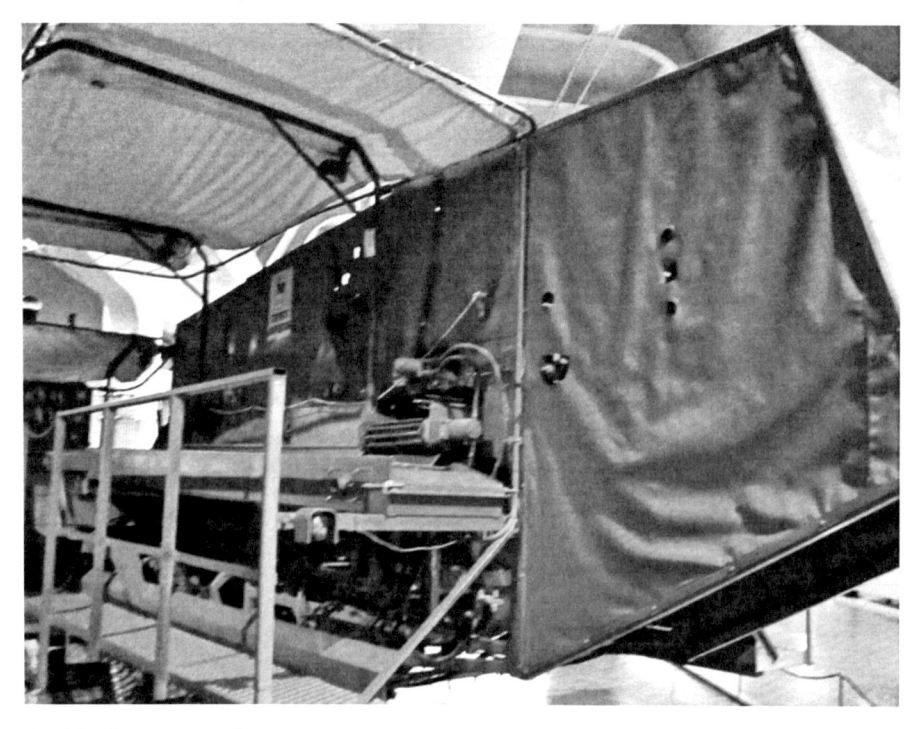

Inside the tomato harvester.

Machines at work

Dan has worked during the tomato harvest on a towed sorter. He says it's hard work.

"All I had to do was grab and get rid of any rotten tomatoes and plant mess, so that only good fruit went up the belt onto the trailer. It sounds easy, but it's messy work as you end up standing on bad tomatoes. I had to work quickly – there could be anything up to twenty objects to check before they moved up the belt. There's no time to think about what you're doing."

"It's noisy work. The harvester is loud and the colour sorter that gets rid of soil and green tomatoes is louder still. You must wear earplugs. You can't hear yourself think, and it's too loud to chat to your workmates. It's dusty work too, though the tent does keep the worst of the dust off. There is a noisy fan that brings in air but it also brings in dust. I thought goggles would help, but they really don't work."

"You're on your feet all day, for as long as 9 hours. In one day we harvested three and a half trailer loads. That's about 45 tonnes of tomatoes! It's very hard work."

Freshly harvested tomatoes ready for the cannery.

Machines at work

Apple picking in the UK is still largely done by hand, especially for eating apples. That's because picking by machine can lead to bruising. Apples that are grown for cider can be harvested by machine though. If the apples are going to be crushed right after harvesting, it won't matter if they bruise when they are picked.

For picking apples by machine, there are three options. Firstly, there are machines the grower attaches to a tractor. These have an arm that holds the tree and shakes it. The apples fall into a set of buckets.

New machines will mean hand-picking is a thing of the past for many cider-apple growers.

Secondly, there are purpose-built mechanical tree shakers. They use a cloth sling to shake the tree. These tree shakers need two operators. One drives the tractor while the other wraps the sling around the trunk of the tree. Using a shaker with a cloth sling is less likely to damage the tree or its fruit.

Robotic pickers are available, but they are not very common. They have robotic arms that pick apples from the tree. These machines aren't 100% reliable because they can't tell whether or not the fruit is ripe, and they can bruise the fruit.

A robotic apple picker.

Machines at work

America has a large citrus industry with farmers growing crops such as oranges and grapefruit mainly for turning into fruit juice. They need to find ways of producing the crop more cheaply so they can compete with fruit imported from other countries. A new citrus harvester has been invented that will be able to harvest a 40kg box of citrus fruit for less than half the current cost. This machine can harvest fruit 15 times faster than doing the job by hand. It works by shaking the citrus tree's foliage and it doesn't damage the fruit.

Checking fruit harvested by the new canopy shaker.

The new harvester looks a bit like a giant hairbrush. It has 3.6 metre long spikes that rotate as well as shake. It's pulled by a tractor continuously moving at 1-2 miles per hour.

The spikes move into a tree's canopy and gently shake it. Fruit falls onto a conveyor belt that carries it to the back of the machine. Then it drops into a self-propelled container that travels alongside the harvester and holds about 5.5 tonnes of fruit. This unit follows the harvester at the same speed. Both the harvester and the transport unit have built-in rubbish removal systems so that leaves and dirt drop to the ground. The machine can be used to pick lemons, oranges, limes and grapefruit.

3.6 metre long nylon rods rotate and shake citrus trees.

Machines at work

Harvesting grapes for wine production has traditionally been done by hand, but grape harvesters are now used in many countries. They are much quicker than working by hand, so if a large vineyard needs to get fruit off the vine fast, a machine is the best option.

A grape harvester is a tall machine that moves over the vines and uses special fingers (or rods) to shake the grapes off the vine. The rods spin round, beating quickly making the vines move back and forth so that the grape clusters drop off. They land on a catching tray and are moved on a series of belts until they reach the cross conveyor that sits high at the back of the machine. As the grapes drop onto the cross conveyor, two large fans blow out all of the waste leaves and twigs and anything else that isn't a grape.

A grape harvester in action.

The fruit carries on along the conveyor to a trailer that travels in the row next to the harvester. Just before the grapes drop into the trailer a high-powered magnet runs over them to remove any metal, such as wire or clips, that may have been caught by the picking rods.

Machines at work

In America a clever idea has been used to harvest cranberries – they are wet harvested. This means that farmers flood the cranberry fields with water and the next day use a water reel to knock the berries off the vines. Because they are filled with air, the berries float to the surface of the water. Then workers wade through the field and gather the fruit together with large brooms.

Once the berries are all in one place they will either be sucked up with a pump truck, or they'll be lifted out on a conveyor belt. The water reels can be harsh on the fruit, so most wet harvested cranberries are used in juice drinks, sauces, or as ingredients in other products.

Harvesters

Water reels in action wet-harvesting cranberries.

Machines at work

Cotton is grown in huge fields and in the past was a very labour intensive crop to harvest. The first machines that were used harvested one row of cotton at a time, but even so they still replaced forty workers. Modern machines harvest up to six rows at once. There are two types of cotton picking machine. One strips the entire plant – picking the lint, which is the part of the plant that is used to make cotton, as well as lots of the plant itself. A process inside the machine removes the lint and puts it in a basket.

The second type of machine, a spindle picker, is a more advanced machine. It was designed by Case working with cotton producers to combine the process of picking the cotton with turning it into cotton bales, known as modules. The spindle picker plucks the cotton from the plant using rows of spiky spindles. The cotton is taken off the spindle with a roller and is put in a basket. When the basket is full the machine squashes the cotton into a module, which is a tight, heavy block. These modules weigh about 21,000kg each and are stored until they are ready to be processed. During processing the seeds are removed and used for cooking oils and the raw cotton is used to make textiles.

Harvesters

A John Deere cotton harvester.

Machines at work

Technical specification – John Deere S690

The John Deere S690 is one of the most powerful combine harvesters in the world.

Power	626 horsepower
Engine	13.5 litre turbo-diesel
Transmission type	3 speeds
Top road speed	18mph (29kph)
Grain tank volume	14,100 litres
Grain tank unloading rate	120 litres per second
Fuel tank capacity	1,250 litres
Price	£280,000
Cutting unit width	9.15 metres
Operating weight	16,585kg (without header)
Tyres	Drive tyres 800/65 R32; Steering Axle Tyres 540/75 R28

Harvesters

The John Deere S690.

Machines at work

Glossary

chaff	the outer layer that is separated from grain before it can be used as food
cider	an alcoholic drink made with apples
continuously	all the time
conveyor belt	a continuous moving piece of rubber or metal used to transport objects from one place to another
debris	broken pieces of something
excess	more of something than is needed
fertiliser	something which is spread on the land or given to plants, to make plants grow well
forage	food supplies for horses and cattle
hopper	a large funnel or container
horsepower/hp	a unit for measuring the power of an engine
imported	goods bought in from another country
ingenious	a very clever new idea
manufacturer	a company that makes large quantities of goods, usually in a factory
mature	a plant that is completely developed or ripe
scythe	a tool with a long handle and curved blade used to cut tall grass and crops
self-propelled	able to move under its own power
textiles	types of cloth made by weaving

threshing	removing the seeds of a crop by hitting it either by machine or hand
traditionally	something that is done in a way that has been carried out for a long time
vineyard	an area of land where grapes are grown